MAY   2008

HIGHLIGHTS OF NASCAR RACING™

THE MOST VICTORIOUS CARS OF NASCAR RACING

JEFFREY SPAULDING

rosen publishing's
rosen
central

New York

For Scott and Bart

Published in 2008 by The Rosen Publishing Group, Inc.
29 East 21st Street, New York, NY 10010

Copyright © 2008 by The Rosen Publishing Group, Inc.

First Edition

Library of Congress Cataloging-in-Publication Data

Spaulding, Jeffrey.
The most victorious cars of NASCAR racing / Jeffrey Spaulding. — 1st ed.
    p. cm. — (Highlights of NASCAR racing)
Includes bibliographical references and index.
ISBN-13: 978-1-4042-1398-2 (library binding)
1. Stock cars (Automobiles)—Juvenile literature. 2. NASCAR (Association)—Juvenile literature. 3. Stock car drivers—United States—Juvenile literature. I. Title.
TL236.28.S66 2008
796.72—dc22

2007037748

Manufactured in the United States of America

On the cover: Dale Earnhardt, one of NASCAR's most celebrated drivers, enjoyed great success racing the #3 car.

CONTENTS

Jeff Gordon's #24 Monte Carlo goes into a turn with the competition following close behind during a NASCAR Nextel Series race at Bristol Motor Speedway, in Bristol, Tennessee. Gordon's multicolored #24 is one of the most distinctive cars in NASCAR.

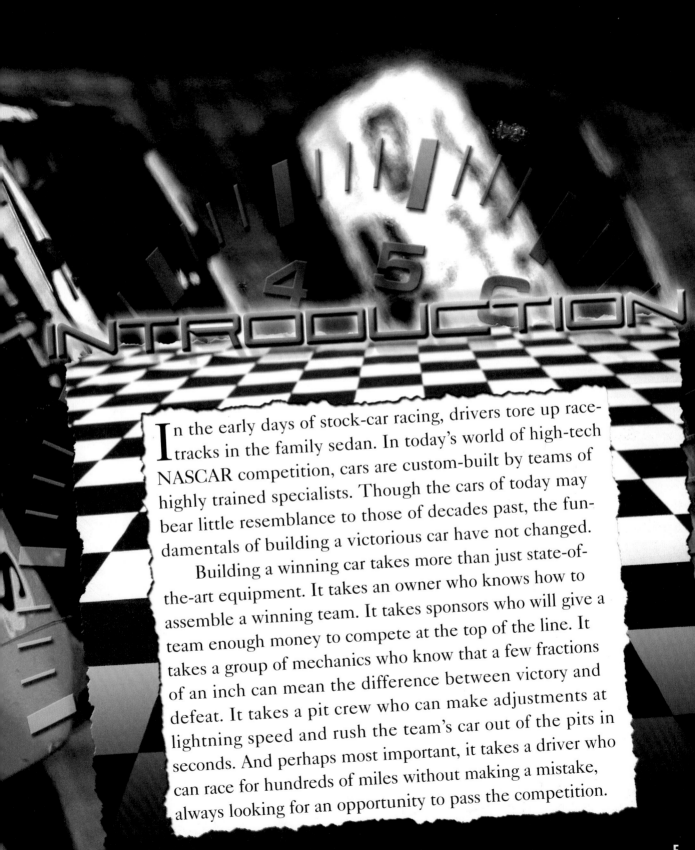

INTRODUCTION

In the early days of stock-car racing, drivers tore up race-tracks in the family sedan. In today's world of high-tech NASCAR competition, cars are custom-built by teams of highly trained specialists. Though the cars of today may bear little resemblance to those of decades past, the fundamentals of building a victorious car have not changed.

Building a winning car takes more than just state-of-the-art equipment. It takes an owner who knows how to assemble a winning team. It takes sponsors who will give a team enough money to compete at the top of the line. It takes a group of mechanics who know that a few fractions of an inch can mean the difference between victory and defeat. It takes a pit crew who can make adjustments at lightning speed and rush the team's car out of the pits in seconds. And perhaps most important, it takes a driver who can race for hundreds of miles without making a mistake, always looking for an opportunity to pass the competition.

THE MOST VICTORIOUS CARS OF NASCAR RACING

The first modified stock cars were used to break the law. From 1920 to 1933, the U.S. Constitution's 18th Amendment prohibited the manufacture, transportation, and sale of alcohol. This period of time, known as Prohibition, resulted in a market for illegally produced alcohol, or moonshine. It was smuggled from place to place in cars specially modified to outrun police. When Prohibition ended, there were a lot of great drivers with incredibly fast cars. These drivers began racing one another informally until "Big" Bill

The cars of NASCAR have gone through great changes over the years. Above, in 1958, stock cars compete at the Darlington 500 in Daytona Beach, Florida. Advances in car design have made stock-car racing both faster and safer.

France established NASCAR (National Association for Stock Car Auto Racing) in 1949.

NASCAR was different than any other racing league in the world. In the beginning, its rules allowed drivers to race only cars that were available on the commercial market. Automotive innovations such as the powerful 1955 Chevy overhead V8 engine or Ford's "W" engine blocks weren't available only to NASCAR drivers. They were available to the public at-large. The fact that the average consumer could purchase the car that his or her favorite racer drove on the track made the sport wildly popular in the United States, especially in the Southeastern states.

Over time, rule changes and safety concerns transformed the stock cars raced in NASCAR competition. These days, stock cars bear little resemblance to street cars. They might look similar from a distance, but their differences become apparent upon closer inspection.

Today's stock cars have a body manufactured out of a thin layer of sheet metal. There are no headlights, taillights, or turn signals. There is only one seat, made out of metal and molded into the shape of the driver's body. The seat is surrounded by a protective cage, which features a state-of-the-art safety harness. Instead of a speedometer, there is only a tachometer. There are no side windows. Instead, protective netting shields the driver from debris.

Decades ago, innovations in engine technology or body aerodynamics could allow a particular car to dominate races. Today, NASCAR rules ensure that no single car model has a huge advantage. Most stock-car models are so similar that impeccable driving and engine setup often determine who is going to Victory Lane.

CHAPTER ONE

Richard Petty and the #43 Car

It is not uncommon for entire families to be involved in NASCAR. In the case of the Petty family, four generations have climbed into stock cars to make their name at the track. The first Petty to race a stock car was Lee Petty, who ran the #42. But it was his son, Richard, who would turn the neon blue #43 car into the most iconic car in the history of the sport. At times, Petty's #43 car was so dominant that officials changed the rules of the sport to level the playing field.

Richard Petty raced the #43 at the front of the NASCAR pack for decades. By seeing how the great #43 cars transformed over time, it is possible to learn about how NASCAR drivers, crew chiefs, mechanics, and pit crews chased victory in the sport's formative years. The story of the #43 car is the story of the sport itself.

The Early Days of #43

Lee Petty didn't allow his son to race stock cars until he was out of his teens. Then he gave Richard a 1957 Oldsmobile—the first #43 car. At that time, virtually none of the stock-car safety features that we know of today were in place. There were no roll bars or restraint harnesses, for example. The cars, including the #43, were truly "stock" cars, identical to cars found on America's highways.

Petty and Plymouth

The first great #43 car was a Plymouth. Richard Petty's fruitful relationship with the automotive manufacturer began in 1960.

The Plymouths that year had a ferociously powerful 383-cubic-inch V8 wedge engine with 330 horsepower, which could reach about 150 miles per hour (241 kilometers per hour). The #43 was 208.2 inches (529 centimeters) long with a wheelbase measuring 118 inches (300 cm). It weighed in at 3,250 pounds (1,474 kilograms), had twin shocks for each wheel, and a three-speed manual transmission. Due to a shortage of white paint for his #43 Plymouth Savoy, Petty mixed in some dark blue paint that was lying around the garage. The paints combined to create a vivid blue unlike the color of any other car on the track. This color became known as "Petty Blue."

Toward the end of 1960, a larger 413-cubic-inch (1,049 cubic cm) engine was introduced. NASCAR had a policy of homologation, which meant that cars had to be sold to the general public in order to qualify for use on NASCAR tracks. NASCAR would eventually abandon this policy, but at the time many drivers' successes could be largely determined by what was rolling out of the automobile factories in Detroit, Michigan. Producing cars that could dominate at the racetrack also benefited the auto industry, since cars that were successful on the track often sold well for street use. Having Petty behind the wheel of a Plymouth was great publicity for the company. The #43 won three races that year, the first in an eventual record 200 wins for Petty.

In 1964 (from left to right), Maurice Petty, Lee Petty, and Richard Petty examine the inside of a new race car. The Petty family is one of NASCAR's most enduring racing dynasties.

Petty Enterprises was a family affair, and Richard's brother, Maurice, and cousin Dale Inman worked in the garage tuning engines. Maurice was the engine-building mastermind of the team, working with Richard for more than 30 years, and Inman would be crew chief until 1981. The team was based in the tiny town of Randleman, North Carolina, which is still the headquarters of the Petty Enterprises race shop.

Over time, with Maurice building the engines, Dale Inman calling the shots in the pits, and Richard behind the wheel, it became clear that the #43 was a car to be reckoned with. And in 1964, with a powerful 426 Hemi engine under the hood, it proved to be an unbeatable force. That year, Petty drove the #43 to a Daytona 500 victory, leaving the competition in the dust. He even ran one lap at 174 mph (280 kph), a great speed in those days. At the end of the season, Petty had nine wins, 43 top-ten finishes, more than $100,000 in earnings, and the Grand National championship.

#43 Takes a Hiatus

In NASCAR, strict rules are in place to ensure that no one driver has an advantage. If one car manages to dominate the playing field, fans begin losing interest. With this in mind, Bill France banned the ultra-successful Hemi engine. Chrysler and the Petty team were not happy. They decided to sit out races until July 1965, when France compromised and allowed the Hemi to compete.

France did not want to compromise on safety, however. The Hemis were such fierce engines that they could push cars past the point of safety. More rule changes were instituted to protect drivers. NASCAR also introduced body templates into the sport. Generally, cars had been built from the frame up, with the sheet-metal body being the last thing added. It was customary for race teams to alter the body shape in order to make it cut through the air more efficiently and go faster. But too much speed could be dangerous. Therefore, NASCAR put a stop to this practice, strictly enforcing proper dimensions for stock-car bodies. Today, body templates are a crucial part of the professional sport.

The Year of the King

Fans knew that Richard Petty was a driver to watch and that Petty Enterprises was an intimidating race team. But perhaps not all of them knew what Maurice Petty was capable of in the garage. In 1967, he made the #43, a 1967 Plymouth Satellite, the fastest car on the track. The #43 weighed 3,500 pounds (1,587 kg) and had a wheelbase of 115 inches (292 cm). Maurice Petty had installed a unique rear differential on the car, which was pushed by a 600-horsepower, 426-Hemi engine under the hood.

Petty's Plymouth that year was legendary. Not only did it win 27 out of 48 races (including a ten-win streak), it also racked up a staggering 38

Richard Petty's #43 car leads the pack in the 1966 Daytona 500. The #43 Plymouth led 108 laps, ultimately beating the cars of Cale Yarborough and David Pearson to win the race.

top-five finishes. Petty won his second Grand National championship and pulled in more than $150,000 in earnings. During a 1967 race in Nashville, Tennessee, Petty crashed the car into the wall, throwing the whole vehicle out of alignment and snapping one of the rear springs. The pit crew stuck in a new spring and did their best to quickly fix the alignment. They had hoped the car might be able to finish the race. By the time he got back on the track, Petty was down by seven laps. The #43 was such a good car that year, however, that he raced it ahead of the pack to ultimately win! From then on, Petty would be nicknamed "the King," and the #43 "Petty Blue" car would be his royal ride.

Good-bye and Hello Again

The Plymouths that Chrysler came out with in 1968 were far less successful. The #43 fared poorly in 1968—so poorly, in fact, that Petty Enterprises defected from Chrysler and went to Ford. This was a major blow to Chrysler, and the company began working on a car that would lure back the greatest stock-car racer in the world. Chrysler would be successful in this goal, producing one of the most famous cars in NASCAR history.

Flight of the Superbird

Officials high in the Plymouth organization would do anything to see the #43 become a Plymouth again. They even went as far as talking directly to Richard Petty, hoping to discover what he wanted out of the company's cars.

The car they created would be one of the most aerodynamic to date. Testing the designs in a wind tunnel, Plymouth engineers came up with a shark-like car with a nose that tapered to a point. The Superbird, as it was called, also featured a spoiler so large that it was essentially a wing affixed to the trunk, pressing the car firmly down onto the track at high speeds. It had a 116-inch (295 cm) wheelbase and weighed 3,841 pounds (781 kg).

The Superbird, however, was unreliable. By this point in NASCAR history, many teams were no longer relying on a single car. NASCAR

Richard Petty enjoyed a long relationship with his sponsor STP (Scientifically Treated Petroleum). Painted in STP red and "Petty Blue," the #43 would become the most recognizable car in NASCAR's history.

raced on different types of tracks: long tracks, short tracks, and road courses. Teams that could afford more than one car were beginning to build cars modified for specific tracks. In 1970, Maurice Petty set up two #43 Superbirds, as well as a #43 Roadrunner for certain tracks. In fact, Richard Petty crashed the #43 Roadrunner at Darlington Raceway in Darlington, South Carolina, nearly killing himself. Although Petty drove to 18 victories in 1970, he finished a disappointing fourth place in the overall standings.

The #43 Rules

NASCAR had benchmark years in 1971 and 1972. It convinced R. J. Reynolds, a tobacco company that manufactured Winston cigarettes, to sponsor the entire racing series. This sponsorship meant that the ultimate prize in the sport would be renamed the Winston Cup. Big money was pouring into NASCAR, and teams were expanding. There was more at stake, more rules, more sponsors—and tougher competition.

The fact that NASCAR quickly passed rule changes to con- strain the winged Superbird didn't affect Petty and his #43 team at all. If anything, it just cleared the field for them to rule the road. The #43 ran laps around the competition in 1971, beginning with a victory at the Daytona 500. Petty ended the season with 21 wins and, ultimately, the Winston Cup championship. Andy Granatelli, president of STP, was impressed. He wanted his company to spon- sor Petty and the #43. This lucrative sponsorship deal came at the right time, since the Chrysler Corporation had made the decision to stop sponsoring NASCAR teams.

A major turning point in NASCAR came in 1972, marking the beginning of the sport's modern era. NASCAR decided to run fewer races in a season, and a new points system was introduced. Entering this new era at the top of the game was the #43—a Dodge Charger painted vivid "Petty Blue" and STP red—one of the most iconic stock cars in NASCAR. With a 426 wedge motor and a 118-inch (300 cm) wheelbase, and weighing in at 3,800 pounds (1,723 kg), the Dodge Charger was a landmark in car design. That year, the #43 cruised to a fourth championship.

The Dodge Charger had a long production run, which meant that Petty was not obliged to change to a different car if he didn't want to. And he didn't: The #43 remained, for all intents and purposes, the same car until 1977. The Charger took back-to-back championships in 1974 and 1975. It never ended a season ranked lower than fifth place.

A Long Reign

The #43 had a winless season in 1978. In 1979, sick of the cumbersome Dodge Magnum they'd been running for the past year, the Petty team decided to switch over to a Chevrolet Monte Carlo. However, as was usual practice for Petty Enterprises, the car was customized and bore little-to-no resemblance to Monte Carlos driven on the street. It was built from both General Motors and Ford parts. Although the Monte Carlo scored only five victories that year, Petty finished first in points, walking away with his seventh championship.

By the time Petty retired from racing in 1992, he had created a racing legacy that no other driver has been able to top to this day:

200 wins, 712 top-ten finishes, seven championships, seven wins at the Daytona 500, and more than $8 million in earnings. The "Petty Blue" #43 remains the most recognizable car in NASCAR history.

#43 *Post Petty*

Petty Enterprises continues to have a healthy existence, even after the retirement of its star racer. Richard Petty's son Kyle drives the #45

Wearing his trademark cowboy hat and sunglasses, Richard Petty rests against the #43 before the 1983 Daytona 500. Petty's friendly demeanor made him a fan favorite.

car, and Bobby Labonte has taken over driving #43. Other racers to drive the #43 following Richard Petty's 1992 retirement include Wally Dallenbach Jr., John Andretti, Bobby Hamilton, Christian Fittipaldi, and Jeff Green.

Sponsorships

Why are today's NASCAR race cars plastered with advertisements? The colorful paint schemes featured on NASCAR racers are the logos of sponsors, who fund race teams. Sponsors are important because NASCAR is such an expensive sport. Each car costs about $100,000. And each race team can have from 12 to 18 cars—every one customized to run on different NASCAR tracks! Stock cars are raced at extremely high speeds, so engines wear out quickly and must be replaced frequently. Each engine costs about $50,000. Racing tires can cost upwards of $1,500 a set; one car may burn through 10 or 15 sets during a race. In fact, simply transporting a car and all its parts around the country can cost hundreds of thousands of dollars. In addition, owners must pay the drivers' and crew members' salaries. All in all, it costs millions of dollars a year to build and maintain a victorious car. Luckily, NASCAR sponsorships provide great advertising for companies. Brand recognition and fan loyalty are much higher for NASCAR sponsorships than for any other

CHAPTER TWO

Dale Earnhardt and the #3 Car

Rule changes, as well as trends in consumer car design, meant that the cars on NASCAR tracks were becoming very different from the cars driven on the streets. Of course, what makes a good race car has always been different than what makes a good street car. Race cars need to be faster, stronger, more aerodynamic, and safer than normal cars. But a major world event also widened the gap between street cars and stock racers: the energy crisis of 1973.

The oil crisis had a major impact on the U.S. automobile industry as well as on NASCAR. The group of nations that produce a majority of the world's oil, OPEC (Organization of Petroleum Exporting Countries), ceased doing business with a number of countries. The price of gas skyrocketed in the United States, and the auto industry responded by introducing more fuel-efficient automobile designs. These new cars could not be easily customized for racing. NASCAR drivers kept driving faster cars that consumed a lot of gas. From that point on, the stock cars used in NASCAR had little to do with those driven by American consumers.

Richard Childress Racing and the #3

In 1979, when Richard Petty was driving the #43 to a final championship victory, a brash young man named Dale Earnhardt won the
NASCAR Rookie of the Year award. The next year, Earnhardt won
the Winston Cup. Despite his early success, Earnhardt would not
truly blossom into a great driver until he hooked up with the racing
team and the car—the #3— that would help define a new era of
American NASCAR racing.

There has been a #3 car since the very beginning of NASCAR.
During the 1949 season, three separate racers drove the #3. Over the
years, many notable racers have found themselves driving a car desig-
nated #3. Fireball Roberts, Junior Johnson, David Pearson, and Cale
Yarborough all drove the #3. In 1976, Richard Childress drove the #3
and stayed behind its wheel for six seasons.

Childress had some success as a driver, but it was as an owner
that he became a NASCAR icon. Earnhardt was his first star driver.
Wrangler, the company sponsoring Earnhardt, followed him to
Richard Childress Racing in 1984. Childress put young Earnhardt in
the #3 car.

A New Approach to Victory

Kirk Shelmerdine led the #3's crew. Shelmerdine had come from
humble beginnings, rising quickly within NASCAR's ranks. He
decided to take a systematic approach to building and maintaining
his cars. He and his crew focused on the specifics of each track and
modified their cars for optimum performance at each race. Engine

Dale Earnhardt, standing with his pit crew, the "Flying Aces," waves to fans after a 1986 race. Earnhardt was one of the greatest figures in NASCAR.

builder Lou LaRosa became a legend in the sport. The #3 car's pit crew, known first as the "Junkyard Dogs" and later as the "Flying Aces," became famous for their highly choreographed, incredibly efficient pit stops. They put Earnhardt back on the road in record times. The "Flying Aces" won pit-crew championships four consecutive years, from 1985 to 1988.

Total Domination

The #3 team's hard work paid off as their car rose to dominate the field in 1986. Behind the wheel of the yellow-and-blue Wrangler-sponsored

Chevrolet Monte Carlo, Earnhardt had finally hit his stride. He established such a vast points lead that, by the final race of the 1986 season, his Winston Cup championship was a forgone conclusion.

That year, the #3 was a 1986 Monte Carlo SS Aero Coupe. The Aero Coupe had a different profile than Monte Carlos from previous years, with a sleek, aerodynamic back that reduced the car's wind resistance. At only a little more than 200 inches (500 cm) long, with a 108-inch (274 cm) wheelbase and a cast-iron V8 engine block, the #3 Monte Carlo would be the car to beat for some time.

The Chevrolet Monte Carlo itself was an incredible car. To this day, the Monte Carlo remains the most victorious brand of car in the sport, its reputation solidly built on its performance during the 1980s. From 1980 to 1989, it took home eight of nine Winston Cup championships. Three of those championships were awarded to Earnhardt in his #3 car.

Flush with cash after his star driver's championship season, Childress immediately poured his winnings back into the #3 team. The #3 took the

Richard Childress Racing

The #3 didn't become one of the most victorious cars in NASCAR because of Dale Earnhardt alone; he rose to the top alongside Richard Childress. Richard Childress Racing (RCR) is one of the most advanced racing organizations in NASCAR. With six to eight people employed in researching and developing new engine designs, and around 60 people employed in manufacturing engines for RCR teams, huge amounts of money are spent to make these cars run as fast as possible.

22

Richard Petty (#43) and Dale Earnhardt (#3) race neck-and-neck at the 1987 Daytona 500. The #3, at the time sponsored by Wrangler and sporting its yellow-and-blue color scheme, would eventually finish in fifth place behind Petty's #43, which came in third.

championship again in 1987, Earnhardt's third. He racked up 11 wins that year, 21 top-five finishes, and more than $2 million in prize money.

The Man in Black

Strangely, Earnhardt's primary sponsor, Wrangler, did not return to sponsor the #3 in 1988. The new primary sponsor, GM Goodwrench, gave the #3 a whole new look. The paint scheme of the car changed from the yellow-and-blue Wrangler colors to a glossy black. The press, who had begun referring to Earnhardt as "the Intimidator" for his ruthless driving style, now had a new name for him: the "Man in Black."

THE MOST VICTORIOUS CARS OF NASCAR RACING

The black #3 Monte Carlo became a fan favorite. Millions of dollars worth of merchandise bearing the #3's distinctive design would be sold over the years.

The Victories Continue

The #3 was unable to coast to a third Winston Cup in 1988. Its team regrouped to rethink their strategies and the car itself. In 1989, the team

The #3 was maintained by one of the best pit crews in NASCAR. Here, the pit crew, headed by Kirk Shelmerdine, swarms around the #3 during a 1991 race. Shelmerdine would eventually go on to try his hand at racing.

Dale Earnhardt and the #3 Car

Bobby Labonte (#18) pursues Earnhardt (#3) during the 1998 Daytona 500. After years of trying, Earnhardt won the race, capturing the one victory that had eluded him for much of his career.

switched to the Chevy Lumina model. The #3 car would remain a Lumina for five more years and 29 victories.

The #3 won two more championships in 1990 and 1991. Shelmerdine, the crew chief who led the #3 to 40 wins, left the team in 1992 to try his hand at driving. The #3's new crew chief, Andy Petree, was on board for Earnhardt's final two championships in 1993 and 1994.

An Elusive Victory

One victory that eluded the #3 team, and Earnhardt especially, was the Daytona 500. The first race of each season, Daytona is also the most popular. Winning the Daytona 500 is a great honor, one that the #3 team felt incomplete without.

In 1998, that would all change. With Kevin Hamlin now serving as crew chief and Danny Lawrence as head engine builder, Richard Childress Racing was prepared to build the best car possible to run at Daytona. Also on board was mechanic and gas man Danny "Chocolate" Meyers, whose humor and down-to-earth personality made him a fan favorite.

Earnhardt and the #3 beat out Jeff Gordon and Bobby Labonte to win the Daytona. The Childress team, and Earnhardt especially, were ecstatic. After the checkered flag fell, Earnhardt drove the #3 into the infield, gleefully doing doughnuts. Every single member of every race crew came out to congratulate Earnhardt and the #3 team that day. The #3 team had finally captured the honor that had escaped them for twenty years.

The #3's Final Ride

Three years later, in 2001, Dale Earnhardt was killed in a crash while driving the #3 in the Daytona 500. Holding off a pack of other drivers while his son, Dale Earnhardt Jr., pushed to take the lead, the #3 lost control and slammed into the wall. NASCAR had lost one of its greatest drivers.

Earnhardt's death prompted major changes in NASCAR, including the implementation of a head stabilizer called the HANS (Head and Neck Support) device and padded walls. It also led to NASCAR's newest innovation, "the Car of Tomorrow." Since his death, the #3 has not been driven. Some say that it will never run on a NASCAR track again.

CHAPTER THREE

Alan Kulwicki and the #7 Car

By the 1990s, NASCAR had become a big-money sport, and large racing organizations such as Richard Childress Racing had dozens of employees. The more rules that NASCAR passed to reduce technology's influence over the field, the more important it became to have a good team and driver. The days of a particular make and model of car achieving total domination over the sport were drawing to a close.

However, even as the cars were becoming more homogenous, teams were still finding ways to be original. Perhaps the most original car in NASCAR's history belonged to a racing misfit from Wisconsin named Alan Kulwicki. His legendary #7 car was nicknamed "the Underbird."

The Underdog

Alan Kulwicki always dreamt of being a race car driver. However, as a Northerner who held an engineering degree, Kulwicki was an unlikely candidate for NASCAR. After racing locally in Wisconsin, he

Alan Kulwicki (inset), both a driver and the owner of his own team, was one of the most ambitious racers in NASCAR. Above, emergency crews attend to Kulwicki and his #7 car after a crash during the 1987 Daytona 500.

decided to leave his life in the Midwest to focus on a career in NASCAR. Kulwicki sold his belongings and headed South.

The greatest drivers in the sport are often from the South, and many grow up behind the wheel of a race car. Therefore, the 30-something Midwesterner—who brought his briefcase to the track and worked on his own cars—stuck out. An independent-minded individual, Kulwicki was not only a driver, but also a team owner. Behind the wheel of the #7 car, he garnered NASCAR Rookie of the Year honors for 1986.

Alan Kulwicki Racing was a relatively small operation, employing a tightly knit crew of just 13 people. The #7 team included crew chief Paul Andrews, team manager Cal Lawson, car chief Tony Gibson, and head engine builder Roy Viccaro. Based out of a small shop in Concord, North Carolina, the Kulwicki team worked hard to build cars that would meet their boss's extremely high standards.

Owner-driver Kulwicki could be a difficult and exacting man to work with, but he understood the effort his small team put into his car. Going up against much larger teams with far greater resources, the #7 team made up the difference through skill and hard work. Kulwicki didn't get the kind of remarkable wins tally that Petty or Earnhardt had before him, but he managed to stay a contender points-wise. After a couple of winless seasons, the #7 won the 1988 Checker 500 in Phoenix, Arizona.

The #7 team was ecstatic, and Kulwicki took his first-ever victory lap—backward. He'd wanted to do something that would make NASCAR fans remember the #7's first victory. It worked. Calling it his "Polish victory lap," Kulwicki waved to delighted fans as the #7 made its way around the track.

The Underbird

Zerex Antifreeze, the company that had been the #7's primary sponsor, left the Kulwicki team in 1990. However, Hooters restaurant soon inked a deal to be the new #7 sponsor, remaining with the team through their only championship.

The year 1992 would prove to be the #7's time. Kulwicki was an engineer, and the #7 team took a scientific approach to the operation of

Kulwicki races in his Hooters-sponsored Ford Thunderbird. Kulwicki and his #7 car competed on a shoestring budget and were always up against tough odds.

Alan Kulwicki and the #7 Car

Nobody thought underdog Alan Kulwicki could drive the #7 to a Winston Cup championship. However, he did so in 1992. At left, after the Hooters 500 race at Atlanta Motor Speedway in Hampton, Georgia, Kulwicki hoists the championship trophy.

its car. Built from a 1992 Ford Thunderbird, with a 113-inch (287 cm) wheelbase and measuring slightly more than 200 inches (508 cm) long, the engine generated more than 700 horsepower. The #7 had a great year, with two wins and 17 top-ten finishes.

Earlier in the season, a collision had erased the "Th" from the "Thunderbird" decal on the front of the car, so it read "Underbird." Kulwicki, NASCAR's longtime underdog who had risen through brains, skill, and sheer perseverance, asked Ford for permission to leave off the decal's "Th" once the car was fixed. Ford assented, and Kulwicki's famous car was thus christened. He even sewed a patch of the cartoon character Underdog onto his racing suit.

By the end of the 1992 season, the points race was tight. At the final race, the Hooters 500 at Atlanta Motor Speedway in Hampton, Georgia, six separate drivers had a chance of walking away with the championship. The #7 team may have been one of the best in the business, but they were up against the toughest competition in the world. Furthermore, the odds stacked heavily against them. They had a $1.7 million budget, about one-tenth the amount of the other teams.

However, they did have several advantages: few of the other teams had a driver who knew his car as well as Kulwicki did and few teams had ever needed to work as hard as the #7 team did.

Victory and Tragedy

The #7 didn't win the race that day. It didn't have to. Calculating how many laps he could run before having to pit, Kulwicki figured out that he could get the most points if he led the most laps. The Underbird finished behind the winner, Bill Elliot, but the #7 had enough points to take the championship. It was the closest championship in NASCAR history and the first to be celebrated with a Polish victory lap.

Just when it looked like NASCAR had a new hero, Alan Kulwicki was killed in a plane crash in 1993, only four months after he'd won the championship. It was a heavy blow for the racing world. Alan Kulwicki Racing continued on without its founder. The Family Channel became the #7

One of the reasons Alan Kulwicki was so successful was that he knew his #7 car inside and out. During a race, communication between the driver and the pit crew is permitted only via two-way radio. Stock cars don't have the ability to relay data back to the crew chief during the race. During practice laps prior to the race, however, about 60 sensors are attached to the cars to collect data about every aspect of the automobiles' operation. The sensors are taken off before the race starts, but the data is analyzed in an attempt to prepare for every possible contingency that might occur during the race. It also makes sure that the cars are set up properly before the green flag is dropped.

Underbird's new sponsor, with Geoff Bodine in the driver's seat. However, Bodine crashed the #7 at Dover in 1993.

By the end of its career, the #7 Underbird had racked up five wins, 74 top-ten finishes, about $5.5 million in earnings, and one hard-won Winston Cup championship. The car had become a true NASCAR legend.

The wrecked Underbird was eventually sold to a pair of racing enthusiasts, who fully restored it to its former condition. It is currently on display at the North Carolina Auto Racing Hall of Fame Museum.

CHAPTER FOUR

Jeff Gordon and the #24 Car

The day that Alan Kulwicki celebrated the #7 Underbird victory in Atlanta was Richard Petty's last day in the #43. It was also Jeff Gordon's first race in the #24. Born in Vallejo, California, in 1971, Gordon was a brash young upstart with his whole career ahead of him. During that race that day, the #24 finished at the back of the pack. Little did anyone know that a new legend was about to be born.

The #24

When Jeff Gordon was young, his family realized that he had a passion for speed. So the Gordon family moved to Indiana, where Jeff would have more opportunities to race. He eventually attracted the attention of Hendrick Motorsports, one of the most successful organizations in NASCAR.

Owned by Rick Hendrick and based out of a large compound in Concord, North Carolina, Hendrick Motorsports has a team of more than 400 employees. Ninety-five people work in the engine department alone! Its size and wealth allow Hendrick to build some of the most victorious cars in NASCAR.

In 1992, the car Gordon stepped into—the #24 Chevrolet Monte Carlo—was built especially for him. With DuPont signed on as Gordon's primary sponsor, the #24 began ascending through the NASCAR ranks.

A young and aggressive driver, Gordon initially had a slight problem controlling the #24. In his eagerness to win, Gordon was pushing the #24 too hard. But the #24 did better every season. Two wins in 1994 blossomed into seven wins in 1995 and the Nextel Cup championship. In 1996, the #24 finished second in the rankings. It won back-to-back championships in 1997 and 1998.

The 1998 #24 earned more than $9 million. It ran on a 358-cubic-inch (909 cubic cm) V8 engine generating 720 horsepower and a Jericho four-speed transmission. With a 100-inch (254 cm) wheelbase and a length of 194 inches (493 cm), the #24 Chevrolet Monte Carlo with the multicolored DuPont paint job was a car that some fans loved—and other fans loved to hate.

The #24 Crew

Jeff Gordon is a great driver, but the #24's success rests just as much on its amazing crew. All NASCAR pit crews have nicknames, and the #24 crew is called the "Rainbow Warriors," after the colorful uniforms that match their car's paint scheme. From 1992 to 1999, Ray Evernham served as the #24 crew chief. Evernham had previously worked for owner-driver Alan Kulwicki. If he learned anything from working with Kulwicki, it was to take a scientific approach to his job.

The DuPont-sponsored #24, driven by Jeff Gordon, races around the track during the 1998 NASCAR Winston Cup at the Daytona International Speedway in Daytona, Florida. (Inset) Gordon celebrates after beating a tough field of drivers to win the 1997 Daytona 500.

As crew chief, Evernham instituted a plan to whittle seconds off the #24's pit-stop time. By running numerous time trials, reviewing video, and making sure everyone was in peak physical condition, Evernham managed to get the Rainbow Warriors' pit-stop times down to the 16- to 17-second range. They practiced frequently and worked out in order to stay in excellent shape.

Evernham left the #24 team in 1999, and Robert Loomis stepped in as crew chief. Replacing Evernham, who was generally considered to be one of the greatest crew chiefs ever, was daunting, but Loomis helped the #24 team cruise to a championship in 2001. In 2005, Steve Letarte replaced Loomis. Letarte, in his mid-20s at the time, had

Above, Ray Evernham, crew chief of the #24 until 1999, maneuvers the car to its starting place before a 1997 race. Driver Jeff Gordon, at right, walks alongside.

worked for Hendrick Motorsports since he was a teenager. Letarte has brought a lot of new ideas to the #24 team, earning praise from Ray Evernham himself.

Hendrick Motorsports

To stay at the top of the game, Hendrick Motorsports puts a tremendous amount of resources toward building the best cars possible.

The engines in the #24 and other Hendrick cars are built by the Hendrick Engine Program, which is staffed by dozens of specialists. They make sure that the engines are running at maximum efficiency.

The #24's engine, for example, is taken apart after each race. The parts are all tested, and those considered still worthy are reconstituted for the next race. It's rare for any engine to last for more than 20 races.

The #24's chassis is assembled in the Hendrick Chassis Department. A new chassis can be manufactured in about a week. The Chassis Department is also responsible for making any modifications to the existing car.

Pit Stop

When a car pulls in for a pit stop, seven people are allowed to jump "over the wall" to work on the car. A gas man runs out to top up the car's gas. A catch-can man comes out to collect any overflow fuel (if any high-octane fuel spills onto the car or track, the car could easily catch on fire). A jack man runs out to jack the car up off the ground. There are two tire changers, each one accompanied by a tire carrier. The pit crew tries to get the driver in and out of the pit stop as quickly as possible. Sometimes, cars come in just for a tire change and to top up their gas. Other times, more involved changes can take place, such as adjusting the car's suspension.

In the early days of NASCAR, pit crews might be drivers' friends or family members. Today, pit stops are coordinated for maximum speed. Many pit-crew members are former professional or college athletes who are hired for their strength, stamina, and speed. NASCAR teams even employ trainers to keep their pit crews in top condition.

Car of Tomorrow

By 2008, the #24—as well as every other car on the track—will conform to a single design. Called "the Car of Tomorrow," the new design will have additional safety features, make races more competitive, and ultimately lower teams' costs. The Car of Tomorrow is slightly less aerodynamic than previous stock cars

The introduction of "the Car of Tomorrow" is one of the biggest changes to occur in NASCAR. No one is quite sure yet how it will affect the sport. Here, driver Elliott Sadler tests the new model car in 2007 at Bristol Motor Speedway in Bristol, Tennessee.

and has a more centralized seat, a smaller fuel cell, and a body that will result in less of a shock for the driver in the event of a crash.

A few Car of Tomorrow races have been run, but it may take several years to assess the new car's true impact on NASCAR. Some people think that the Car of Tomorrow will take some of the fun out of the sport. But one thing is certain: like all NASCAR transformations meant to narrow the gap between teams, the Car of Tomorrow will highlight the roles of pit crews, drivers, and engine builders. In a sport where success is sometimes measured in a thousandth of a second, human skill is more important than ever.

GLOSSARY

aerodynamics The study of how air flows around objects in motion. Engineers use aerodynamics to build cars that will go through the air easily and quickly.

catch can A special can used by the pit crew during pit stops. It is used to collect the extra, very flammable gasoline so it won't spill onto the ground or car.

chassis The skeleton or framework of the car, over which all other mechanical parts will be attached.

crew chief The leader of a race car team, in charge of the pit crew and mechanics, as well as ensuring that a race car functions perfectly during a race. The crew chief also makes most technical decisions during a race, like when a pit stop is necessary and what adjustments to make.

defect To leave a group or organization and join its rival.

differential The part of a car that allows it to turn. Specifically, the differential lets a car's axles rotate at different rates during a turn.

homogenous Similar, or the same, in nature.

homologation A NASCAR policy that required every race car be a real "stock car," which consumers could buy for street use.

horsepower A unit of measurement used to describe how much power an engine puts out. NASCAR race cars use much more horsepower than street cars.

iconic Relating to somebody or something that is admired.

pit crew The team of mechanics who maintain and repair race cars during races. In NASCAR, every team is allowed to use seven pit-crew members.

roll bars Tubular steel bars that surround the driver inside the car. Roll bars prevent the driver from being crushed in the event of a roll.

shock absorber In simple terms, a shock absorber absorbs sudden shocks when a car's tires drive over an uneven surface. This guarantees a smoother ride and helps ensure that the car—and the driver—are not damaged or injured.

spoiler A piece of metal attached like a small shelf on the back of a race car. It creates a small window for air to rush through, which pushes down on the back of the car and keeps it on the track.

stock car A race car based on the body design of a car available to the general public.

tachometer A meter that measures the engine's number of revolutions per minute.

template A long metal mold that fits over a race car and is used to make sure that a race team has the officially approved dimensions for their car model and hasn't made any illegal modifications.

wheelbase The distance from a car's front axle to its rear axle. Cars with short wheelbases are faster and can turn more quickly, while cars with long wheelbases are more stable but slower.

Motorsports Hall of Fame of America
P.O. Box 194
Novi, MI 48376-0194
(800) 250-RACE (7223)
Web site: http://www.mshf.com
The Motorsports Hall of Fame hosts exhibits on some of the best
drivers in stock-car and open-wheel racing, as well as motorcycling,
drag racing, sports cars, air racing, and power boat racing.

NASCAR Technical Institute
A Branch Campus of UTI of Arizona, Inc.
220 Byers Creek Road
Mooresville, NC 28117
(866) 316-2722
Web site: http://www.uticorp.com
The exclusive educational partner of NASCAR, this institute is a
technical training school that combines a complete automotive
technology program and a NASCAR-specific motor sports program.

National Association for Stock Car Auto Racing, Inc. (NASCAR)
P.O. Box 2875
Daytona Beach, FL 32120
Web site: http://www.nascar.com
NASCAR is the official sanctioning body for stock-car racing in the
United States. It consists of three major national series (the Nextel
Cup, Busch, and Craftsman Truck series), as well as eight regional series.

Richard Childress Racing (RCR)
425 Industrial Drive

Welcome, NC 27374

(336) 731-3334

Web site: http://www.rcrracing.com

The RCR organization was the first to win championships in the Nextel
Cup, Busch, and Craftsman Truck series. The RCR museum is
located on the RCR campus. It houses almost 50 racing vehicles, a
large number of which are #3 cars driven by Dale Earnhardt Sr.

The Winston Cup Museum

1355 N. Martin Luther King Jr. Drive

Winston-Salem, NC 27101

(336) 724-4557

Web site: http://www.winstoncupmuseum.com

This museum preserves NASCAR history and Winston-Salem's ties to
the sport. Displays include authentic race cars from different eras
of Winston Cup history.

Web Sites

Due to the changing nature of Internet links, Rosen Publishing has
developed an online list of Web sites related to the subject of this book.
This site is updated regularly. Please use this link to access the list:

http://www.rosenlinks.com/hnr/vica

FOR FURTHER READING

Burgess-Wise, David. *The Ultimate Race Car Book*. New York, NY: DK Adult, 1999.

Burt, Bill. *Stock Car Race Shop: Design and Construction of a NASCAR Stock Car*. Osceola, WI: MBI Publishing Company, 2001.

Burt, William. *Behind the Scenes of NASCAR Racing*. Osceola, WI: MBI Publishing Company, 2003.

Craft, John Dr. *Classic Stock Cars*. Osceola, WI: MBI Publishing Company, 1997.

Hammond, Jeff. *Real Men Work in the Pits: A Life in NASCAR Racing*. New York, NY: Rodale Books, 2006.

McReynolds, Larry, and Jeff Huneycutt. *How to Become a Winning Crew Chief*. Phoenix, AZ: David Bull Publishing, 2005.

Miller, Timothy, and Steve Milton. *NASCAR Now*. Buffalo, NY: Firefly Books, 2004.

Newton, Tom. *How Cars Work: An Illustrated Guide to the 250 Most Important Car Parts*. Vallejo, CA: Black Apple Press, 1999.

Woods, Bob. *NASCAR Pit Pass: Behind the Scenes of NASCAR*. Pleasantville, NY: Reader's Digest, 2005.

BIBLIOGRAPHY

Aumann, Mark. "Car No. Histories: No. 3." NASCAR.com. February 12, 2004. Retrieved June 2007 (http://www.nascar.com/2004/news/headlines/cup/02/12/car_history_3/index.html).

Aumann, Mark. "Enduring Performance: 1988 Checker 500." NASCAR.com. April 18, 2006. Retrieved June 2007 (http://www.nascar.com/2006/news/headlines/cup/04/18/belliott.ep.phoenix/index.html).

Beam, Larry. "1992 Winston Cup Championship 'Underbird.'" Underbird.com. Retrieved June, 2007 (http://www.underbird.com/undrbird.htm).

Burt, William. *The American Stock Car*. St. Paul, MN: MBI Publishing Company, 2001.

Craft, Dr. John Albert. *Classic Stock Cars*. Osceola, WI: Motorbooks International, 1997.

Gabbard, Alex. *NASCAR's Wild Years: Stock-Car Technology in the 1960s*. North Branch, MN: CarTech, Inc., 2005.

Hinton, Ed. "Kulwicki's Legacy Continues Across NASCAR Nation." *Orlando Sentinel*. March 23, 2003. Retrieved June 2007 (http://www.underbird.com/news/33003.htm).

Holder, Bill. "NASCAR Racing—Decades of Change." *Stock Car Racing*. June 2006. Retrieved June 2007 (http://www.stockcarracing.com/featurestories/scrp_0606_nascar_racing/).

Huneycutt, Jeff. "A Day in the Life." *Stock Car Racing*. Retrieved June 2007 (http://www.stockcarracing.com/featuredvehicles/scrp_0510_richard_childress_racing/index.html).

Kallmann, Dave. "Wheels of Fortune." *Milwaukee Journal Sentinel*. November 15, 2002.

McCarter, Mark. "10 Years After: The Points Race Isn't as Tight as It Was in 1992, but—Like in '92—a New Generation of Drivers Is Taking Over at the Top." *Sporting News*. November 11, 2002.

Mulhern, Mike. "Gordon Has Come a Long Way Since 1994."
Winston-Salem Journal. May 1, 2007. Retrieved June 2007 (http://
www.journalnow.com/servlet/Satellite?pagename=WSJ%
2FMGArticle%2FWSJ_BasicArticle&c=MGArticle&cid=
1173351021600&path=%21sports&s=1037645509200).

Nice, Karim. "How NASCAR Race Cars Work." How Stuff Works.
Retrieved June 2007 (http://www.howstuffworks.com/
nascar.htm).

Redgap, Curtis. "Which Came First, the Plymouth or the Petty?"
Allpar.com. Retrieved June 2007 (http://www.allpar.com/racing/
petty-plymouth-racing.html).

Smithson, Ryan. "Shop Remains a Reminder of Kulwicki Racing."
NASCAR.com. April 1, 2003. Retrieved June 2007 (http://
www.nascar.com/2003/news/headlines/wc/03/31/kulwicki_shop/
index.html).

Stewart, Ben. "NASCAR's Controversial Car of Tomorrow, Here
Today." *Popular Mechanics.* April 2007. Retrieved June 2007
(http://www.popularmechanics.com/automotive/motorsports/
4212811.html).

Wise, Jeff. "NASCAR Goes High-Tech." *Popular Mechanics.* March
2005. Retrieved June 2007 (http://www.popularmechanics.com/
automotive/motorsports/1336277.html).

INDEX

THE MOST VICTORIOUS CARS OF NASCAR RACING

About the Author

Jeffrey Spaulding is a writer and researcher based in New York State. He was first introduced to the excitement that is NASCAR by his older brothers and has since become an ardent fan of the sport.

Photo Credits

Cover, pp. 4–5, 25, 28 (inset), 30, 36 © Getty Images; p. 3 © www.istockphoto.com/Jason Lugo; pp. 6, 12 © Time & Life Pictures/Getty Images; pp. 10, 21, 24, 31 © AP Images; pp. 14, 28 © Focus on Sport/Getty Images; pp. 17, 23, 37 © George Tiedemann/GT Images/Corbis; pp. 18, 22, 32, 38 © www.istockphoto.com/Simon Podgorsek; p. 39 © Getty Images for NASCAR.

Designer: Nelson Sá
Photo Researcher: Cindy Reiman